Don't Lose Your Identity

John 1:12

"But as many as received him,
To them gave he power to become the sons of God,
Even to them that believe on his name."

Also by Ella J. Alexander:
Encourage Your Own Heart
The Mind of a Warrior
Seeing Without Seeing – Faith Connection

Printed in the United States of America

First Printing, 2017

ISBN-13: 978-1974354054
ISBN-10: 1974354059

All scriptures included in this book are in King James Version.

Table of Contents

Acknowledgement

First and foremost I give praise, glory and honor to God, who is the Head of my Life; to my Lord and Savior Jesus Christ, who is the Savior of my soul, and to the Holy Spirit who is my leader and guider into all truth and the path of righteousness. The God-Head is the lover of my soul, my deliverer and healer. I wouldn't be who I am without God.

To my two sons, Malik and Roddell. I love you both.

To my Overseer, Apostle Levar Williams and Associate Pastor: Prophetess Jeanette Williams along with the entire Dominion Family you know that I love you all very much.

Dedication

I dedicate this book to all of those who are struggling to find out who they are in Christ or just have forgotten who they are in life.

To my late dad, Raymond Alexander. As always I wish you were here to share this moment with me.

Introduction

Separate Ways

We have walked together
Many, many years;
Because of you, I have experience so much pain
And shed so many tears.

I allowed you to lead me into doing things
That I should not have done;
You had me thinking and believing
That those things I participated in was fun.

Now I sit back
And just reminisce on those days
I thank God and I'm grateful because
One of us decided to go our separate way.

Though the other still comes back
Refusing to let the old relationship be,
It had to come that one day of us
Had to open our eyes to finally see.

If I would have stay with you;
No doubt, I would have decayed.
That's why, Satan! God has strengthen me
To turn my back to you and go my separate way.

April 8, 1999

Don't Lose Your Identity

CHAPTER 1

The Beginning: *The Process*

When a baby is born, the first step that is to be performed is to immediately cut the umbilical cord and place a wrist band with the last name on it on the baby's wrist. This wrist band, along with the mother's wrist band should match each other. That is how the child is identified with the mother. The second step is to draw blood and have the blood tested; not only for diseases, but also for drugs, abnormalities, infections, and blood type. The third and final step is the birth certificate, which is very important. This step includes giving the baby a name in which he or she would be known by. Sometimes the child may have the mother's last name, or

1

either the father's last name. On this document you have one or both of the parents name, place and time of birth. The Birth record proves that the child belongs to a particular woman and man. From that moment, the child has now received an identity.

In the early stages of the child's growth, people will say to one of the parent, "That is your child", "He or she acts just like you" or "He or she looks just like you." The older people say, "Yes, that child reminds me of you when you were growing up." People will acknowledge or testify to whom the child belong and resembles, but as the child continue to grow, the flesh develops as well and sometimes began to do things that are not of the parent(s). The child began to show a different character; different behaviors other than the parent's character in which he or she had inherited.

2

During the growing years, sometime, children will forget who they are and try to be someone else, but only to find themselves later in life seeking to find their own identity. Not knowing who they are, they began to wonder and are lost both spiritually and naturally.

Do you...**Know Your Identity?**

Don't Lose Your Identity

CHAPTER 2

The Blood Process: *DNA*

Please understand that your identity can not be slapped on you. You can't get it from staples, Walmart, Macy's, or the Nike Store. You can't walk into the Olive Garden, Captain George, or the Cheesecake Factory and order an identity. In order to be identified, we have to go through a process called the Blood Process. The blood process tells who your father is. Romans 8: 12-16 says,

[12]Therefore, brethren, we are debtors, not to the flesh, to live after the flesh.

[13]For if ye live after the flesh, ye shall die: but if ye through the Spirit do mortify the deeds of the body, ye shall live.

[14]For as many as are led by the Spirit of God, they are the sons of God.

[15]For ye have not received the spirit of bondage again to fear; but ye have received the Spirit of adoption, whereby we cry, Abba, Father.

[16]The Spirit itself beareth witness with our spirit, that we are the children of God:

So the two questions that must be asked is, 1) did you go through the blood process? And 2) how many of us know to whom we belong?

Yes, I know many of us want to say God due to fact that He created everything. We want to say God is our Father because He was in the beginning before the very beginning of creation and way before the start of man. Some of us said, God, when we were asked "Who is your father?", but when the test results came back, it had on it,

Don't Lose Your Identity

DNA. That meant that the blood did not agree with your confession. It did not mirror what you put down on paper. DNA – Did Not Agree. *Oh, don't drop your head now.* I hope that your jaw didn't drop on that one; but it's the truth.

There is no escaping this process. It must be performed. Just like in life you can't have two biological mothers and fathers; it goes the same in the spirit. You only have one Spiritual Father. You CAN NOT have two. There is nowhere in scripture where God said we had two spiritual fathers or could have two spiritual fathers.

So at the end of this process, the result of the test is revealed. It is either you are born of God or not. There is no in the middle. There is no fence to straddle. One side of you cannot be black and the other side white. I am sorry. It just doesn't work that way. Romans 8:9 says,

7

"But ye are not in the flesh, but in the Spirit, if so be that the Spirit of God dwell in you. Now if any man have not the Spirit of Christ, he is none of his." Simply put: YE MUST BE BORN AGAIN

The blood process has never failed. It reveals the truth and will not compromise. So if you told the truth in the beginning, then the results of the test will be in your favor; but if you lied, then the results will expose you for who you are.

CHAPTER 3

The Problem: Choice

Many are probably wondering where is the problem or if there really was a problem. I know you are asking, "Didn't God create everything well and just the way he wanted it? Did not God give man an identity?" Yes, to all of those questions. When God gave man (generally speaking) an identity, along with it came free will.

What is free will? Free will is the choice to choose; freedom; to power to act voluntarily without constraint.

Free will is not the problem. The problem is what and who we choose. Because we have a right to choose what we want and who we want, whenever we want, God has

9

instilled in us the ability to know right from wrong with the slight assistance from ADAM. *Thank you, Adam (sarcastic thank you).*

God does not have anything against our right to choose; the problem God has with us it that we choose what goes against His will concerning us. We choose people rather than Him. We choose to worship things and other people instead of worshipping Him. We choose to love others more than we love Him. So, again, it is not our right to choose that was the problem; it was what and who we chose. When we choose to go against the will of God and disobey God that was *the problem.*

When most people start to speak of sin in the beginning automatically they find it with Adam, but what

10

about us? What about all of our choices? Even children have a certain amount of understanding between right and wrong. They aren't born completely dumb, not knowing anything. Look at Jacob and Esau who were fighting inside of the womb of Rebekah, who was Isaac's wife (Deuteronomy 25:19-27).

Do you understand how you can lose your identity now? It didn't just fall off of you. Neither did someone steal it. We made a choice to leave it unguarded. We basically gave it away and were left with nothing. We were left in a state of confusion and in that state there is no good thing. Just problem after problem; one right after the other. We don't see it until it is too late. When I say that it is too late, I mean that there is no time to try to lock doors, or hold onto it and pull it back. There is no putting a safety lock. The word of God says, *"Then when*

11

Don't Lose Your Identity

lust hath conceived, it bringeth forth sin and sin, when it is finished, bringeth forth death." – James 1:15). Lust of the eyes is what has been getting man in trouble for a very long time. Because we lust and end up sinning; we were destined to Hell. So the only thing and option we have is God, who is the Alpha of our Identity.

Again, it is not the right to choose that is the problem; it was our choice that became the problem. Look at this if you don't believe me.....

People who utilized their right to choose and end up making the wrong decision.

Adam and Eve: Eve went off and didn't consult her husband after speaking with the snake. Adam chose to listen to Eve over God, (Genesis 2:15-18; 3:1-13, 17-

12

24). **The result:** They experienced a spiritual death AND got evicted from their home. Take note: They were the first homeless couple.

Moses and the Children of Israel: The people murmured and complain. They cried for something to eat; God gave them manna. They begged for water; God gave them water. The first time God told Moses to strike the rock and the water come out of it. The second time God told Moses to speak to the rock, but Moses struck it. Moses allowed the complaints and ungratefulness of the people get next to him and he ended up choosing to strike the rock to take out his frustration, (Exodus 17:1-7; Numbers 20:1-12). **The result:** He was not allowed to enter into the promise land that was full of milk and honey.

David and Bethsheba: The lust of David's eye was for another man's wife. Because he chose to have her and be with her; when she became pregnant, David then had her husband, Uriah, killed (2 Samuel 11 – 12:24). **The results:** God took David's newborn son.

Peter and Jesus: Jesus told Peter that the time would come that he would deny him. Peter never ever thought that he would be in denial about Jesus because he loved Jesus so much that he was willing to die with him. However, after Peter chose to deny Jesus; realization hit him when Jesus looked up on him and his words came back to his remembrance (Luke 22:34, 56-63; Matthew 26:34). **The Result:** Peter ran away and repented.

Cain and Abel: A well-known story about two brothers. Abel was the one that offered up a sacrifice pleasing unto the Lord and his brother, Cain, didn't. So

14

Cain chose to murder Abel and thought he would g

away with it and God wouldn't know. How silly?

(Genesis 4:1-16). **The result:** Cain was cursed and a

marked was placed upon him. He was a fugitive and a

vagabond in the earth.

Sampson and Delilah: The great and almighty

Samson of Gaza, a Nazarite, fell in love with a Philistine

woman named Delilah. The lords of the philistine of the

city harassed Delilah to find out the source of Samson

strength.   When Samson chose to tell her after she

inquired two other times; this time, which was the third

time…, he finally gave in and told her his secret that no

one was supposed to know (Judges 16:1-31). **The**

result: The people cut of Samson hair and he lost his

strength. They captured him, poked out his eyes, put him

in prison, and offered him up as a sacrifice to their God.

d restored his strength to avenge the poking out his eyes, Samson died along with the rest of the people.

Aaron and his two sons, Nadab and Abihu: Aaron is the same person that walked with Moses. There came a time when Nadab and Abihu decided to offer up strange fire unto God. Aaron would never do such a thing. (Leviticus 10:1-6). **The result:** God killed them both immediately.

Those following people made a choice and the choice was not pleasing to God. The results were not pretty at all. So that is a lesson for us that in our right to choose, we must choose wisely.

CHAPTER 4

THE ADOPTION:

How many of us know of someone who had been adopted due to circumstances or situations beyond their control? Adoption is a good thing because what a person is actually saying is "I know this is not my child, but I am willing to adopt him or her into my family. They are willing to give that baby or child a new identity because he or she will now carry the last name of the adoptive parents. The adoptive parents begin to teach and feed and care for the child. They watch over the child for years.

Now the scripture says, *"For ye have not received the spirit of bondage again to fear; but ye have received the Spirit of adoption, whereby we cry, Abba, Father."* We have been adopted by God because we were born into sin and shaped in iniquity. If you don't believe me, here it is in the word of God: *"Behold, I was shapen in iniquity, and in sin did my mother conceive me."* – Psalm 51:5.

As a baby we knew nothing about the sin that waited for us to arrive. When I say arrive, I am speaking in the womb; the complete formation... after the baby is totally developed. Now after the baby have come out of the womb, that is when all the action begins to take place that we could see with our own eyes. Now, as babies, we don't remember opening our eyes, nor our first words or our first step. But we do remember the things that we did later on as we got older. You know those things that

18

many act as if they are proud about doing this very day or just claim it's a habit and have to stop doing sooner or later? Yea, those exact things that is being done: smoking, cursing, lying, stealing, sleeping with our best friend's girlfriend or boyfriend, having sex outside of marriage, murder and the list goes on and on.

We all were in a state of NO RETURN. No man could help us. By that time, we couldn't be identified by anyone. Not even our so called friends could identify us. Some of us could hear the people saying and whispering, "He used to be a well-mannered child. She used to be so beautiful. She used to look like her mother, but God help her. He used to be a handsome young man, just like his dad, Father God have mercy on him." We had lost our identity and didn't even know it.

Some of us didn't know what to say or do. Thank God that many of us were given back to God at a very young age so even when we messed up, God yet took us in and cleaned us up. For the rest who were able to confess that we were a hot mess and wreck; we could utter the words "Jesus Save Me." God hears the cries of those who are sincere. We were washed in the blood and made whole. Because of the adoption and the blood, we had a brand new start. We had a new family. We had a new name and a new look. We now and once again had an identity, but this identity was in Christ Jesus.

So thank God for the Blood that was shed on Calvary. Thank God for the life that was laid down for our sake. We must thank God for saving a wretch like us. We were and still are undeserving of it. But God who is rich in mercy saved us and made all things become new and our old life was passed away.

Just because we have been adopted into Christ, we have to keep in mind that when we give and commit our lives unto the Lord, it is the Spirit of God that bears witness that we are children of God. We have God's Holy Spirit within us. He begins to teach us and led us in the paths of righteousness (Roman 8:14; John 16:13). We began to love. We began to have compassion. We began to do and walk upright before the Lord. We want to be more like Christ. We start desiring to have the mind of Christ (*"Let this mind be in you, which was also in Christ Jesus"*, Philippians 2:5). We now have a connection, a relationship with God because we have been born again (John 3:5-7 *"Jesus answered, Verily, verily, I say unto thee, Except a man be born of water and of the Spirit, he cannot enter into the kingdom of God. That which is born of the flesh is flesh; and that which is born of the Spirit is spirit. Marvel not that I said unto thee, Ye must be born again.")*

CHAPTER 5

Knowing Who You Are

Our identity distinguishes us from every other person on the face of the earth. There is no two of you. Even identical twins aren't really identical because if they were, then that would be a problem. Everything about them would be the same...finger prints, foot prints, etc. The reason God created us the way He did is because our identity joins us together with the one that created us. The one that is identical with the one that saved us. The Son and the Father...they are the same in every possible manner. It is imperative that we KNOW WHO WE ARE.

Although we discuss knowing our identity; it is even more important that we know who we are and from whom we came. In whom we live and have our being. If we don't know who we are; then would our identity matter?

The Bible tells us in Romans 8:17 that we are heirs of God and joint heirs with Christ.

Galatians 4:7 says, *"Wherefore thou art no more a servant, but a son; and if a son, then an heir of God through Christ.*

When we receive Christ in our lives, we are adopted into the Spirit. We are transformed into a living spirit because Christ paid for our freedom with his own blood. He purchased us for His very own purpose. After the Spirit of adoption, we were called Children of God (Romans 8:14) because we now had received an identity.

24

Not only that. God didn't stop there. The Spirit of God began to teach us, lead us, and guide us into all truth. We were trained to be warriors of God. We ARE more than conquerors in Christ Jesus. When we know to whom we belong, and we can declare our identity, we can boldly acknowledge that we are God's disciples, his ministers, deacons, elders, evangelist, pastors, prophets, teachers, and apostles. We are followers of Jesus Christ. We are no longer unknown one to one another. We recognized our sisters and brothers in Christ because of our identity amongst one another, because of the unity and love of Christ, and because of the mercy and grace of God, because of the Holy Ghost that dwells in each of us.

CHAPTER 6

Know Your Identity

When we KNOW who we are in Christ, we can go anywhere that the Spirit leads us. Do whatever the Holy Spirit tells us to do and accomplish that which we were commanded to accomplish in the name of Jesus.

So how important is it for us to know our identity? It is the utmost importance. No one can tell us better than the Word of God.

Genesis 1:26, "And God said, Let us make man in our image, after our likeness."

It is a great honor to know and receive the truth that God wanted us to be made in the image of the Trinity. He wanted us to be like the Father, the son and the Holy Spirit. So for the many of you that don't know who you are or who you came from, I am here to let you know that God created you. God designed you from the very crown of your head to the very soles of your feet. He knows all about you because you came from Him. Stop allowing people to tell you that you came from a monkey. THAT IS A LIE FROM THE HEART OF HELL AND THERE IS NO TRUTH IN IT! We all came from God, a Spirit that has been given a soul and we live inside of a body.

Plenty of people don't know or appreciate who they are because they think more of others than themselves. There are some people that believe that God created some of us to be better than others, or the rest of the generations, but not so.

We ought to be thanking God right now at this very moment for thinking of us…for being mindful of us.

Stop walking around here feeling ashamed of how you look, or how you are shaped because of someone else negative and narrow-minded opinion. Be proud of who you are. God's word says that we are peculiar people. So don't put on a mask. Stop piling on make up trying to make yourself look like someone else or stand in the shadow of someone who doesn't even know you exist. If you are going to stand in anyone's shadow, let it be God's shadow. He knows where you are at, where you are going, how you feel, what you like, what makes

29

you ill so forth and so forth. God did not create any junk. Everything he created, he blessed it because He loved what he saw.

My sisters and my brothers...please let us stop thinking that we are less of a person because of certain qualities or qualifications that the world (our enemy) may have and the saints of God don't need. Whether you are saved or not, I need you to understand and accept that we all have specific qualities and characteristics. For those that are saved, they have the qualifications they need because it was given to them and begin to manifest when and after they gave their life to Christ and they should know their identity. If you are not saved, know that you still have an identity, but it is up to you to know who you are. Don't try to be someone that God didn't make you to be. If you want to be great, get to know God and then you will know that you are of God and that you ARE

somebody. If you know who you are and whose you are;

You Know Your Identity.

CHAPTER 7

What does God say about your identity?

Gen. 1:26-27 *"And God said, Let us make man in our image, after our likeness: and let them have dominion over the fish of the sea, and over the fowl of the air, and over the cattle, and over all the earth, and over every creeping thing that creepeth upon the earth. So God created man in his own image, in the image of God created he him; male and female created he them."*

John 1:12 *"But as many as received him, to them gave he power to become the sons of God, even to them that believe on his name:"*

Romans 6:6 *"Knowing this, that our old man is crucified with him, that the body of sin might be destroyed, that henceforth we should not serve sin."*

1 John 3:1-2 *"Behold, what manner of love the Father hath bestowed upon us, that we should be called the sons of God: therefore the world knoweth us not, because it knew him not.*

2Beloved, now are we the sons of God, and it doth not yet appear what we shall be: but we know that, when he shall appear, we shall be like him; for we shall see him as he is."

Galatians 3:27-28 *"Knowing this, that our old man is crucified with him, that the body of sin might be destroyed, that henceforth we should not serve sin."*

1 Corinthians 6:19-20 *"What? Know ye not that your body is the temple of the Holy Ghost which is in you, which ye have of God, and ye are not your own? For ye are bought with a price: therefore glorify God in your body, and in your spirit, which are God's.*

1 Peter 2:9 *"But ye are a chosen generation, a royal priesthood, an holy nation, a peculiar people: that ye should shew forth the praises of him who hath called you out of darkness into his marvelous light:"*

1 Corinthians 6:17 *"But he that is joined unto the Lord is one spirit."*

Jeremiah 1:5 *"Before I formed thee in the belly I knew thee; and before thou camest forth out of the womb I sanctified thee, and I ordained thee a prophet unto the nations."*

CHAPTER 8

Don't Lose Your Identity

Time after time, we experience things in life and we are drained. We are pulled on from every side. Everyone wants us to be this and to be that. Behave or act this way, act that way, and all of this behaving and acting takes away from who we are. Others aren't paying attention to the person who we were designed to be. At the end of the day, we are feeling lost and hopeless. All we know is that we go to Church; we have a family or a loved one, and a job we don't care to show up at. Outside of that, what can we tell them about us? I'm not referring to race; because many of us don't even know our race

35

because we are too busy trying to be another race. Why don't take a moment and ask yourself, "Who am I?"

You are more than flesh and blood. You are more than someone's brother or sister. You are more than another social security number. Remember, your identity. Understand who you are.

There were times we were involved with someone and we were so focused on them, we forgot about us. We no longer existed. We can't keep losing ourselves in circumstances, situations, games, heartbreak, other people selfishness, etc. It is time for us to know us. It is time we get back our identity. You matter just as much, even more so than any famous actor or singer. We don't have to be on stage or in front of the camera. Neither do we have to be on TV. The most important people are those who go unnoticed.

36

Your voice matters, your thoughts matter, your opinions matter, but with all the riches in the world, it wouldn't mean anything if you don't know who you are. You have to know that you are important. God designed you that way. You have to know that you have a purpose in the world and it is not to be someone's carpet or mat.

If you don't know your purpose, ask God. Surely He will tell you. Don't walk around like zombies from a video game. Don't be someone's puppet, they pull your string and you dance. No! Today, God is saying that you were made in His image and after His likeness. You are born of Him. You have His DNA. Don't lose your identity for the cares of this world. They will not help you to recognize your potential in the earth. Tell yourself that after reading this book, You will know who you are and you will hold onto your identity that the enemy tried

to steal from you and the world tried to blind you from.

Chapter 9

This is what the Word of God says about us!

2 Corinthians 5:17 - Therefore if any man [be] in Christ, [he is] a new creature: old things are passed away; behold, all things are become new.

1 Peter 2:9 - But ye [are] a chosen generation, a royal priesthood, an holy nation, a peculiar people; that ye should shew forth the praises of him who hath called you out of darkness into his marvellous light:

Ephesians 2:10 - For we are his workmanship, created in Christ Jesus unto good works, which God hath before ordained that we should walk in them.

Romans 8:1 - [There is] therefore now no condemnation to them which are in Christ Jesus, who walk not after the flesh, but after the Spirit.

John 1:12 - But as many as received him, to them gave he power to become the sons of God, [even] to them that believe on his name:

2 Corinthians 5:21 - For he hath made him [to be] sin for us, who knew no sin; that we might be made the righteousness of God in him.

1 Corinthians 6:19 - What? know ye not that your body is the temple of the Holy Ghost [which is] in you, which ye have of God, and ye are not your own?

John 15:5 - I am the vine, ye [are] the branches: He that abideth in me, and I in him, the same bringeth forth much fruit: for without me ye can do nothing.

Romans 12:2 - And be not conformed to this world: but be ye transformed by the renewing of your mind, that ye may prove what [is] that good, and acceptable, and perfect, will of God.

1 John 4:4 - Ye are of God, little children, and have overcome them: because greater is he that is in you, than he that is in the world.

1 Corinthians 12:27 - Now ye are the body of Christ, and members in particular.

John 15:15 - Henceforth I call you not servants; for the servant knoweth not what his lord doeth: but I have called you friends; for all things that I have heard of my Father I have made known unto you.

Who Do You Look Like?

My actions and my words,

I am who I am...you heard!

I can do what I feel and say what I need,

You speak as if I need to take heed.

I walk amongst the living as well as the dead,

Some people think they are always spiritually right
without any doubt within their head.

I change not for anyone,

I say I am of Christ, the son.

So if I don't want to be bothered with you,

I'm gonna walk away and do as I am led to do.

When I humble myself to my Father,

it only makes me fight harder.

I can't do what you do, or say what you say,

I must be about my father's business and on my way.

42

So when you look at me, who do you see?

Do you see Jesus, the devil or little ole me?

I decided to look in the window that revealed the essence of me,

I finally realized and now I know; that I look like the one that created the spiritual me.

by Ella J. Alexander
February 16, 2011 at 12:53am

Things to do to help keep your identity

1) Identify righteousness and pursue it.

*"But seek ye first the kingdom of God, and his righteousness; and all these things shall be added unto you. **Matthew 6:33***

2) Live Holy for He (Christ) is Holy

"For God hath not called us unto uncleanness, but unto holiness." **1 Thessalonians 4:7**

"But fornication, and all uncleanness, or coveteousness, let it not be once named among you, as becometh saints". **Ephesians 5:3**

"Wherefore come out from among them, and be ye separate, saith the Lord, and touch not the unclean thing; and I will receive you."

3) Do the Will of God

"Love not the world, neither the things that are in the world. If any man love the world, the love of the Father is not in him. For all that is in the world, the lust of the flesh, and the lust of the eyes, and the pride of life, is not of the Father, but is of the world. And the world passeth away, and the lust thereof: but he that doeth the will of God abideth for ever." **1 John 2:15-16**

4) Do unto the Lord and be faithful

?One man esteemeth one day above another: another esteemeth every day alike. Let every man be fully persuaded in his own mind.

He that regardeth the day, regardeth it unto the Lord; and he that regardeth not the day, to the Lord he doth not regard it. He that eateth, eateth to the Lord, for he giveth God thanks; and he that eateth not, to the Lord he eateth not, and giveth God thanks. For none of us liveth to himself, and no man dieth to himself. For whether we live, we live unto the Lord; and whether we die, we die unto the Lord: whether we live therefore, or die, we are the Lord's." **Romans 145-8**

5)Renew your mind and know that you have been changed because of Christ.

"For to be carnally minded is death; but to be spiritually minded is life and peace. Because the carnal mind is enmity against God: for it is not subject to the law of God, neither indeed can be. So then they that are in the flesh cannot please God. But ye are not in the flesh, but in the spirit, if so be that the Spirit of God well in you. Now if any man have not the Spirit of Christ, he is none of His. And if Christ be in you, the body is dead because of sin; but the Spirit is life because of righteousness." **Romans 8:6-10**

6) Read...Study....Read and read some more.

"Study to shew thyself approved unto God, a workman that needeth not to be ashamed, rightly dividing the word of truth." **2 Timothy 2:15**

7) Pray to God and never stop.

"But shun profane and vain babblings: for they will increase unto more ungodliness. **2 Timothy 2:16**

45

"Pray without ceasing" **1 Thessalonians 5:17**
"And he spake a parable unto them to this end that men ought always to pray, and not to faint," *Luke 18:1*

Watch ye therefore, and pray always, that ye may be accounted worthy to escape all these things that shall come to pass, and to stand before the Son of man." **Luke 21:36**

Praying always with all prayer and supplication in the Spirit, and watching thereunto will all perseverance and supplication for all saints." **Ephesians 6:18**

8) Allow God to transform you like He want.

I beseech you therefore, brethren, by the mercies of God, that ye present your bodies a living sacrifice, holy, acceptable unto God, which is your reasonable service. And be not conformed to this world: but be ye transformed by the renewing of your mind, that ye may prove what is that good and acceptable, and perfect will of God. **Romans 12:1-2**

9) Keep Your Clothes on and learn to fight.

"Finally, my brethren, be strong in the Lord, and in the power of His might. Put on the whole armour of God, that ye may be able to stand against the wiles of the devil. For we wrestle not against flesh and blood, but against principalities, against powers, against the rulers of the darkness of this world, against spiritual wickedness in high places. Wherefore take unto yo the whole armour of God that ye may be able to withstand in the evil day, and having done all, to stand. Stand therefore, having your loings

46

girt about with truth, and having on the breastplate of righteousness; And your feet shod with the preparation of the gospel of peace; Above all, taking the shield of faith, wherewith ye shall be able to quench all the fiery darts of the wicked. And take the helmet of salvation, and the sword of the Spirit, which is the word of God:" - ***Ephesians 6:10-17***

10)Hold on to your faith in God and don't let go

"Now faith is the substance of things hoped for, the evidence of things not seen." – ***Hebrews 11:1***

But without faith it is impossible to please Him: for he that cometh to God must believe that He is, and that He is a rewarder of them that deligently seek Him. – ***Hebrews 11:6***

The Identity Prayer

Father, I come before you as humble as I know how. I ask for forgiveness of each and every sin that I have committed knowingly and unknowingly. Father God, I ask of you today that you would hear my plea. I have forgotten who I am in you. I have lost my identity and I need you to restore me. Restore my character, my love, my faith and my joy that you have so graciously given me. Father help me to be the person you created me to be. I am asking to be transformed. I am asking for you to take me in again; again into your bossom; again in your loving arms. Help me to be the child that you speak of. I have lost my way and my sight. I call upon you for help and deliverance. I believe you are able to do all things; therefore, I commit myself into thy hands. I want to be more like you. This is ask in Jesus name, Amen.

Thank you, Father!!

This logo belongs to Victorious Living Faith Ministry in Brooklyn, N.Y.; founder Ella J. Alexander and can't be duplicated.

Made in United States
North Haven, CT
02 March 2023

33446593R00036